MW00881315

NEVER TOO BROKEN FOR GOD

George Shankool

Copyright © 2022 by George Shankool
All rights reserved.

Contents

Opening Prayer

Father God, we thank you for your word, your greatness, your provisions, and your blessings. We give you all honor and praise, you are Almighty, holy, and, above all things. We're so grateful that you have delivered us out of the pit of hell, where we had placed ourselves through our disobedience.

Without you, our lives were filled with selfishness and regret, but because of you, your glory, your faithfulness, and your majesty, you were willing to pay our debt for us. You came down from heaven, you were born as a man into your creation, and were willing to die for us because you knew that we could never pay the debt that we owed.

In the person of Jesus Christ, you lived a life of perfection and obedience. You did not deserve death, but still willingly walked to the cross on our behalf. You bore the sins of the world, past, present, and future and you paid our debt with your precious blood. You have shown your perfect love to your creation in a way that is unexplainable with words. We are so grateful and humbled, and we are in awe of your presence.

Father, we pray that you may continually fill us with your Holy Spirit, that you may guide us, and if we stumble, please lift us, and help us walk back to the cross in humility and repentance. May you continuously help us to keep our eyes fixed on you. Guide our minds and our hearts to stay focused on eternity, and not on this world. May we take the time, talent, and treasure you have given us and use them for your Glory. Let us use them to help others and build up the Body of Christ. May we walk as ambassadors for you, shining a light on the TRUTH you have revealed within the Holy Scriptures. May we show the world the love that you showed us. LORD, please help us to be kind to each other, loving, and forgiving, and give us self-control. Strengthen us and give us the courage we need to spread your Gospel to the world.

LORD, please allow us to walk in unity with our brothers and sisters in Christ. Let us not be burdened by our past, but instead encourage us by knowing that your love was so great, that you were willing to forgive us such a great debt. Please allow us to have understanding and appreciation for your Grace so we may have the motivation to share our testimony and be a witness to the broken world. We are eternally grateful to be covered by the blood of the Lamb, clothed in His righteousness in your sight. We give you all love, honor, and praise, and pray that you may continue to use us and guide us, for your Glory, until the glorious coming of our Lord and Savior Jesus Christ. It is in His name that we come to you in prayer.

Amen, and Amen.

Introduction

Iam so grateful that God led you to this book. I pray that it is beneficial to your growth and your walk with Christ. God moved me to write this to help those of us who have struggled with the extreme brokenness of our past. Those of us who struggle with our past life choices, regrets, and shame. The purpose of this book is to remind every one of us that we are loved and have the opportunity to be forgiven by God through Faith alone in the sacrifice of Jesus Christ. And that He wants to use us for His purposes, regardless of our past.

We have all made mistakes, we have all fallen, and we have all felt alone at times. What we must always remember is that everyone needs God's love, guidance, grace, and forgiveness. Some of us may have been in darker places than others, but the separation from God that we experienced was equal, regardless of how awful we were.

Scripture tells us that there is no one who is righteous, no not one (Romans 3:10). It also says that no one seeks God on their own accord and testifies that we have all sinned and fallen short of the glory of God. Every single human being deserves God's wrath because we have ALL disobeyed Him.

I think some of us see others from a non-biblical lens. While observing and judging others, we seem to have forgotten that the standard for righteousness according to the Bible is God's perfection. And if we are being honest with ourselves we know that none of us can ever reach that standard.

But thanks be to God that He was willing to come down from His throne in heaven, to be born in a manger, humbling himself as a servant, and was willing to pay the price for our disobedience. We could never have paid that debt, but He willingly took on that debt and paid it for us!

This is just about the time that Satan leans in and whispers in our ears, "He's only saying all that nice praise Jesus stuff to you because he doesn't know what you've done.", "God can't forget what you've done!".

Well.... you're right! I don't know what you've done.

But I do know this, the blood of Jesus Christ can cover the sins of ALL people. And when we accept Christ as our Lord and savior God forgives and forgets our sinful past (Psalm 103:12, Isaiah 43:25, Romans 8:1, 2 Corinthians 5:21). And if you want some more scriptural proof, all you need to do is look at the people that God has used throughout Biblical history.

Noah got drunk and ended up naked; Moses killed somebody. King David had an affair, and then had the husband of the woman he was sleeping with killed. Abraham used his wife as a shield and put her in harm's way allowing her to be taken by Abimelech because he pretended, she was his sister, not his wife... Oh yeah, he did that on two separate occasions! Peter denied Jesus three times and even swore an oath saying he never knew HIM, even though he was one of the disciples in Jesus's inner circle. Paul murdered Christians and was hell-bent on stopping the spreading of the Gospel and snuffing out Christianity as a whole.

Good luck topping that!

The stories could go on, and on. There is not anything that we could say or do that would justify us thinking or feeling too broken for God to use. That statement alone is ridiculous... If God is God, he can fix all things, there's nothing outside of His power, and He can use anyone for His Glory.

If we are serving a so-called "god", that is incapable of ALL things, we need to throw that so-called "god" in the trash.

Because a "god" like that is not the TRUE almighty God of the Bible... We serve the God of Abraham, Isaac, and Jacob, the creator of ALL things, the one TRUE living and Eternal God.

All right, now that we got that cleared up, we can all recognize the fact that every person needs the grace, love, and forgiveness of God. We can start moving forward, into what God called us to do. And we will finally be capable of letting go of our past, and understanding who God truly is. We will be able to get into His word and begin walking in a way that would bring glory to Him. We can finally realize that God did not need us, but He wanted us. And we can begin using our past as a testimony to relate to others who are lost and broken. We can encourage them and open the door to relationships, so we can spread the Gospel to them and watch God do for them what He did for us!

Chapter 1

From Death to LIFE!

From Death to LIFE!

My spiritual journey has been a rollercoaster ride, to say the least! I will give you a little background on myself to start this off. I come from a family of believers that have extremely strong faith. Both my mother and father raised me and my sister to love God and honor him in ALL that we do. I have believed in who Christ is, as far back as I can remember, but unfortunately, my actions did not reflect that.

I remember after coming to the Lord, I was reading the Bible and came across a Passage in Matthew 7:21-23 "Not everyone who says to me, 'Lord, Lord,' will enter the kingdom of heaven, but the one who does the will of my Father who is in heaven. On that day many will say to me, 'Lord, Lord, did we not prophesy in your name, cast out demons in your name, and do many mighty works in your name?' And then will I declare to them, 'I never knew you; depart from me, you workers of lawlessness."

WOW!!! That is an eye-opener, Jesus told those people that He never "Knew" them...Meaning that even though they claimed to know Jesus with their mouth, their hearts were not Truly with Him.

I also remember the first time I read James 2:18-19 "Show me your faith without deeds, and I will show you my faith by my deeds. You believe that there is one God. Good! Even the demons believe that—and shudder."

Wow! What a slap in the face to my pride and arrogance that was....

I thought it was "good enough" that I recognized the existence of God and the Truth about Jesus. Unfortunately, I seemed to have missed the repent, confess and believe part of the Gospel.... I realize now that having head knowledge of Truth is very different from fully accepting that Truth in your heart. I had Mental Knowledge of God, but my heart was far from Him.

Am I saying that if you are a TRUE believer in Christ, you will be perfect and will never stumble?

By no means!

But what I am saying is that I only had head knowledge of Jesus and was participating in, and celebrating in, very sinful behaviors. At that time in my life, Jesus was nothing more than a side thought. I will say that I did feel some guilt and conviction. But it was never enough to stop me from doing what I wanted....

Was I just a rebellious Christian living a Carnal life of disobedience? Maybe...

But I can say this for sure, after giving my life to Christ and walking by the Guidance of the Holy Spirit I now feel deep conviction over even the smallest of stumbling. I feel major conviction if I unleash a harsh word on someone, I exhibit a spout of anger, tell a lie, or if I don't share the Gospel with others...

Maybe that came with Maturity in my walk, or maybe I had never fully accepted Christ before...

Only God knows, but either way, I am forever grateful that He called me, forgave me and saved me by the blood of Jesus Christ, and has brought me to where I am now!

Now that we got that out of the way let's get into my story from Death to LIFE!

Let's do a quick recap, I grew up in a Christian home, I knew of God but didn't seem to truly Know HIM. Let's start when things started to shift for me while I was walking on the path of destruction. As I reached my teenage years, I chose to follow a path that was not in any way shape, or form a reflection of how I was raised. I wish could claim ignorance, but instead, I can only admit arrogance. So many believers I meet today have similar stories of debauchery, but very few had the childhood and life I had. I was a special type of awful. I had a great family, great life, and knowledge of the true LIVING God....

I made the conscious choice to run away from God, and the path He had set for me because I thought I knew better. I felt guilt and shame, but I still chose to continue to stray from God's path. I never stopped believing in who God was. But unfortunately, I put him in the back of my mind and refused to serve Him.

Maybe it was because I knew that my shame and guilt would have been amplified 1000-fold if I thought about God.

I could try to blame my friends and their influence, but that's just a pathetic excuse. They never forced me to do anything I didn't want to. I chose to do it freely, and even if I felt "peer pressure", I still had my God-given free will, it was always my choice.

Throughout my teenage years, I got involved in drugs, violence, and crime. Money, power, and pride were at the forefront of my life. I wanted to be the "biggest and the baddest" in everything that I did. I didn't think or care about the consequences of my actions, let alone the repercussions my actions had on the people around me. I assaulted people, stole, threatened, intimidated, destroyed property, other extremely incriminating activities and so much more!

At the age of seventeen, my family and I moved from the metro Detroit area to Phoenix, Arizona. It should have been a good move for my life because I had left all my "old friends", and my "old life" behind. Well, that wasn't the case... I now realize that although I left my friends behind, the main reason for my problems came with me...

If it isn't obvious, I am saying that the root of the problem was me and my sinful nature.

That reminds me of what my father used to say, "You will never escape your problems, no matter how far you run, when the problem is you, and your choices".

By the age of nineteen, I had done more and seen more than most people can even imagine. I had committed criminal acts that could have and should have landed me in prison. I was mixed up with people who were the lowest of the low. My life was filled with gangs, drugs, sex, and violence. I was always very smart, but unfortunately, I was too smart for my own good. I abused the gift of intellect that God had given me to find creative and better ways to make more money doing bad things.

Needless to say, that talent became very popular with the group of people I chose to associate with.

Looking back, I remember always having this "inner voice" speaking to me urging me to change. I felt this overwhelming urge to repent, but I never was willing to do it. Now I see that it was God calling me. He knew my heart, even though my outward actions were not matching what He saw in me.

Well…. Thank God He judges the Heart!

Too many times we see people who look "Righteous", but their hearts are filled with toxicity. I guess we do not have to look too far in scripture to see that either… Jesus was constantly berating the religious leaders who looked righteous, but their hearts were filled with hate, pride, and greed. He would call them, "whitewashed tombs!", clean on the outside and dead on the inside. He also called them, "Hypocrites!", meaning they were only acting righteous.

On the other side of that aisle, is where we often would find Jesus. He went to the sinners of the world and hung out with them, ate with them, and spoke to them about repentance. He taught them God's Truth and many people came to love Him, repented, and followed Him.

Hey!! That sounds like my life! Jesus came to me while I was deep in my sin, He convicted my heart, called me into repentance, and told me to follow Him!

The problem was, I wasn't listening...

So, He had to get my attention in let's say a slightly more impactful way. It took Him allowing my life to be turned upside down and shattered, because of my own doing, for me to finally hear His call.

It was a Friday evening in July of 2001, I was with a friend hanging out, driving around, looking for girls, and acting like... Well... Idiots!

After a night of partying, it was getting late. I started to have a bad feeling and wanted to go home. But my friend wanted to cruise around a little while longer. I reluctantly agreed. When we headed to cruise around town once more, my friend wanted to stop at the gas station because he was thirsty. I agreed and we stopped to grab some water. I decided to stay in the car while he was getting it. I was approached by a young kid around 14 years old, he came up to my driver's window.

He asked me "what's your problem!?"

I explained that I didn't know him, and didn't have a problem, but he insisted that I did....

Just then he made his hand resemble the shape of a gun, stuck it in my face, and said, "Bang! You're DEAD!".

That's when my friend came out of the gas station. He saw someone at my window and ran to the car. As he tried to jump in, we were approached by another person, he was maybe 15 years old. He was trying to pull my friend out of the passenger seat while I was backing out of the parking spot, but he was unable to. We both knew that these kids didn't want to fight, and they must have had guns on them because there was no way they would ever confront us without them. We were way bigger than them and would have had no issue beating them down.

Here is a little backstory.... My friend and I always carried guns when we went out because we were doing bad things and hanging out in bad areas.

Hey, Don't Judge!!

I have already established the fact that I was a pretty big piece of garbage.

Anyway, that night I had this feeling to tell him that we didn't need our guns. I said they were just a distraction, and we were not going out to cause any issues so why bring them...

Well looking back, I see God stopped us from having Guns with us. If I did have them, those kids would have been dead and I would be writing from prison, and I would not have learned what God was teaching me.

Ok, back to the story. We put the pedal to the metal and took off!! They peeled rubber and started to follow us.

That's when I noticed a police car at the intersection. I decided to do a "doughnut" in the intersection to try to get the officer's attention, in hopes he would pull us over. I figured he would scare away the people chasing us. Unfortunately, he must have noticed we were being chased and ignored what I did.

Honestly, I don't blame him. He probably didn't want to put himself at risk. We were in a really bad part of town.

I peeled out and started flying down the street trying to get away from them. I hit the OnStar button in my Cadillac and contacted the police as we were being chased at an excess of 125 MPH on the main streets. We were flying down the street, blowing through red lights, trying to get away, and just then we heard, "BANG!, BANG!, BANG!, BANG!" gunshots! They are now continuously shooting at us as we FLY by another police officer, and still no help! Just then my back window gets shot out, "CRASH", and I hear a scream!

My friend had been SHOT!

He was looking backward when they shot through the back window, the bullet hit his face. It went through his cheek, broke his jaw, and was lodged next to the artery in his neck.

Bullets are still flying; I am yelling at the police dispatchers on OnStar and blood is everywhere!

This was the time I realized that I was not going to survive the night.... Just then, I had this overwhelming urge to pray.

I didn't pray for me to survive because I felt that I didn't deserve God's forgiveness. I had chosen my path and I deserved everything that was happening to me.

Instead, I prayed for my family; I knew they didn't deserve to live with the pain of my poor choices. I asked God to help them Get over my death, to give them strength, and to watch over them.

I accepted the consequences of my choices... I apologized to God for all that I had done and asked Him again to help my family cope with my murder.

Just then I felt this overwhelming feeling that God was urging me to swerve hard to the left and try to make an impossible right-hand turn at 125 mph.

So, I did!

The people chasing us were in an SUV and would have flipped if they followed this crazy turn. I counted in my mind, 3-2-1, TURN!!

The tires are screaming, smoke from the road is filling the intersection, my car is sliding, I think we are going to make it.... Crash!

We hit the curb and ripped the wheels off my car, we slid across the street, sparks were flying, and we kept sliding for what seemed like a hundred feet or more. The people chasing us had not attempted to make the turn, but they were slowing down and trying to come back to finish what they started. I grabbed my friend and dragged him from the car to a car dealership right next to where we crashed. I hid him under a car where they wouldn't find him because I knew if they came back for us, he could not run. I jumped the fence and hid until the police arrived.

Obviously, since I'm sharing my story with you today, I survived, and thank God, so did my friend. But in a way, I did DIE that day! I died to my old self, the lost, broken version of me died, and I was born again. That night was the night I was called by God to follow Him. From that day forward I cut off all of my old friends and dove deep into God's word. I spent my free time reading the Bible from cover to cover, several times over. I knew that I was forgiven and saved by God, and I owed him a debt that I could never repay. I wanted to learn everything about Him, through prayer and the study of His Word. I was done trying to be who I was and finally wanted to become the person God created me to be.

It has been a very long time since God called me, but I remember it like yesterday. I have finally come to accept my past. I used to regret that I had been through so much and would struggle with the fact that I hadn't followed God in obedience my whole life.

Obviously, lifelong obedience is far better than disobedience.

But that is not my story... This is!

God used my terrible past to bring me to this present. He allowed me to fall because of my own choices so He could lift me up. Through my weakness, He was able to show His strength. God has continuously been able to use my troubled past for His good purposes. He allows me to use my brokenness as a tool to mentor so many people who are struggling and broken.

God uses my weakness and my past to show others that they are never too broken for Him to use for His Glory. God helped me to focus my mind, time, and talents on running my family's restaurant, growing the business and using it as a ministry to show God's goodness to our employees, our customers, and our community.

God brought me from death to Life and He allows me to use my past as a testimony to those who have a hard time relating to "Normal Believers". They can feel connected to me, because of my flaws, my past, my brokenness, and my openness to admit my faults. Because of this, they are more open to hearing about the Truth of the Gospel and the promises of God.

I am so blessed that God gave me another chance, even though I didn't deserve it. But in reality, none of us do!

The Bible says that ALL have fallen short of the Glory of God, and ALL have sinned. We are only saved by the Grace of God, through faith in Christ alone, not by our works so none of us can boast!

Since coming to the Lord, God has blessed me with an amazing wife, three beautiful children, and a thriving business. But most importantly a sense of purpose and peace knowing that He saved me, with the purpose to talk to others about Him. I now know that I am part of God's family. The Bible says we have been adopted as sons. I have witnessed His LOVE, and Grace firsthand. I'm so grateful to know that Jesus died once and for all, for ALL the sins of those who put their FAITH in what HE has accomplished, through His death on the cross, His resurrection, and ascension to the right hand of the Father. I know my sins have been wiped clean by the blood of Jesus and now I spend my time reminding other broken people, that we are all humans, and we ALL make mistakes. Some of the greatest men in the Bible had stumbled greatly, Abraham, King David, Moses, Jonah, Peter, Paul, and many more!

But there is Good News!

God has a plan for redemption and it is the offer of salvation to ALL humanity by the Blood of Jesus Christ, for the forgiveness of sins, past, present, and future!

Chapter 2

Sinners Saved by Grace

Sinners Saved by Grace

Nobody, let me repeat that... NOBODY is outside of the Grace of God! Jesus shed His blood for the forgiveness of ALL people. We first need to be humble enough to admit we need forgiveness. Next, we must be willing to turn away from our sinful life and accept His offer of forgiveness and Salvation.

I think we as people like to separate each other into categories where some of us are better than others.

Unfortunately, that comes from the religiosity that has been spewed into society throughout history. You know the teachings I'm talking about. It is that teaching that says there is some sort of separateness among people. Like some are more holy than others, or some distinction between the people that are "good", and those who are "bad".

Well, that's a complete misrepresentation of who people are.

The Bible testifies that ALL people are sinners and we have ALL fallen short of the glory of God (Romans 3:23).

It doesn't say some of us are better than others... It says, if you have broken one law, you've broken them ALL (James 2:10) and deserve God's wrath (Romans 6:23).

The Bible also tells us that the law was given to us to point out the fact that we could never be righteous on our own (Romans 3:20). It was to show us that we are failing daily at what God held as the standard for good....

Good in God's standard is His perfection.

I think one of the biggest disservices that has been done to Christianity is the allowing of the spread of the heresy that there are "good", and "bad" people.

Jesus himself said, "no one is good but God" (Luke 18:19).

If people are good, or even capable of being good, why did Jesus need to die for our sins?

That ridiculousness gives us a false understanding of who God is. We know that God is a God of love, mercy, patience, and faithfulness. We can see that shown in how God was willing to come down, be born as a man (Colossians 1:16), and pay for the sin that we as His creation committed. The debt that we owed Him because of our disobedience was our life (Romans 6:23, Genesis 2:17), both physical and spiritual (Ephesians 2:1-10). God knew that we would never be able to pay that debt, so he willingly came down to be born into His creation, to pay the debt that we could not (1 Peter 3:18). That debt needed to be paid by a man because it was owed by a man (1 Corinthians 15:20-28).

But since no man could live a perfect life to pay for the sins of all, God had to pay that debt Himself. Jesus was able to be born sinless by virgin birth through the power of the Holy Spirit (Matthew 1:23, Isaiah 7:14, Genesis 3:15) In Genesis 3:15 you can see clearly that the woman was promised a child that would defeat Satan, and that Child would be from her "Seed". In the Hebrew language and understanding, we know that was about Christ's virgin birth because men have the seed (Sperm) and women do not. This Passage is often called the first Gospel or "protoevangelium".

This is how Jesus was able to be born without sin. Since the sin of Adam was passed on through the "seed" of man. He also was able to live a sinless life and by doing so, He was the only one capable of paying for the sin of all mankind by His death (Romans 5:8, 1 John 2:1-2). He conquered sin on the Cross, releasing us from the spiritual death that we would have had to face. And by the grace of God through faith in Christ's finished work on the cross, we are born again by the power of the Holy Spirit (John 3:5). We are sealed by the Holy Spirit as a guarantee of our inheritance of eternal life (Ephesians 1:13-14).

We also know that Jesus conquered our physical death through His resurrection. This is how He released us from the power of death, both spiritual and physical.

What does that mean for us? Well, it means that our physical body will still die, but our soul will live on, and even more so, we will be resurrected into new heavenly bodies that do not suffer the curse of death and are imperishable. The Bible says that we can rest assured, because of Jesus's Resurrection (Romans 6:9). We are told that His resurrection is our proof that He conquered both spiritual, and physical death. (1 Corinthians 15:20-22)

Let's take a second here to Praise God for His love, grace, mercy, and forgiveness!

Okay most of us get that. But if God is a God of love, why does He need to punish people? Why didn't He just forgive everyone? Why did somebody need to pay for our debt?

Well, I'm glad you asked!

We can see that scripture testifies that God is the God of justice, and wrath, He cannot lie, and He is faithful. We must combine all His personality traits to see the full picture of who He truly is.

When the fall of Man happened, the entirety of creation was cursed (Genesis 3:17, Romans 8:22). Death was promised to all mankind, because of the disobedience of both Adam and Eve.

We know that God cannot be a liar; so, he had to stay true to His word from Genesis 2:17, and therefore death had to come to His creation, both spiritual, and physical. Just as Adam first experienced spiritual death, by being separated from God in the garden (Genesis 3:23-24). We too have that spiritual separation from birth. Next is our physical death, which comes at the end of our lives, just as it did for Adam.

If we truly want to see God's grace, we need to look at His abounding Love and Sovereignty. God knew before He created any of us, that we would choose to be disobedient and rebel against Him and His law. He knew that we would have to face death because of that disobedience and knew that there was only one way to save us from it...

Having the foreknowledge of what we would do, God showed His great love for us by still choosing to create us, and still giving us the Free Will to choose.

In all reality, God could have chosen not to create us at all. Or given life to only those, He knew would follow and believe in Him. But because of His abounding Love, He gave the opportunity and gift of life to ALL people. Even though He had the eternal foreknowledge of who we would be, and what we would do beforehand.

By still giving the gift of life to all people, He would eliminate any questions of our Free Will. And with that foreknowledge, He knew that we would need redemption and that He would be the only one capable of redeeming us by His blood being shed for us on the Cross.

WOW!!! There is no greater example of SELFLESS LOVE, GRACE, and MERCY.

But we also know that is not the fullness of God's character; Justice, Righteousness, and Wrath are also equally part of God. And those of us who reject His offer of redemption, atonement, and Salvation through the work of Christ on the Cross are rejecting God's LOVE, FORGIVENESS, PROMISES, and SACRIFICE.

Let's look at this in perspective; If an Earthly King were to offer to cancel all our debts to his society so we could escape life in prison or even the death penalty, would we graciously accept that?

Of course, we would!!

We would humbly accept that forgiveness and bow before him, graciously thanking him every day of our life!

But what if we rejected that King's offer?

That is obvious, we would have to pay the debt we owed, with our freedom and our life!

Well, we know from the testimony of scripture that the King of Heaven and Earth offered that same clemency to us. And not only has He canceled our debt to His society, but He paid for it with His blood!

God created all people knowing that we would all fall short of the glory of God (Romans 3:23) and that we would all be condemned (Romans 6:23), but He loved the idea of Mankind so much, that even before He created us, He was willing to come up with the redemption plan to save us, by becoming one of us (Ephesians 1:4). He was willing to suffer and die on our behalf because He also knew on the third day, He would raise Himself from the dead, conquering both sin and death on our behalf. By doing so He became the firstborn from death into the resurrected eternal life (Colossians 1:18). Which has now given us proof of our redemption by His Blood and opened the door to our adoption as sons (Ephesians 1:5), by the grace of God through faith in Jesus Christ. He earned our redemption for us, and we are not saved by our good works, but only through His (Ephesians 2:8). His promise to become co-heirs into eternal life is accessible to ALL who believe (Romans 8:17).

We can now clearly see that scripture says that we are ALL sinners saved by grace.

Chapter 3

Jesus has the wheel...LET GO!

Jesus has the wheel...LET GO!

If you've been walking with the Lord for any amount of time you've probably heard the phrase, "Jesus Take the wheel". I have always found that phrase funny... I would say that in a way that makes more sense biblically. The moment that we come into faith; we are called to submit our lives fully to Christ (Matthew 16:24-26). So, in essence, if you're a believer, Jesus has had the wheel the whole time.

I sometimes picture Jesus yelling at us to "LET GO!!!".

Imagine yourself driving down the freeway, your child is in the backseat, and you're in full control. Your main goal is to protect them from all the dangers that the road can throw at them and get them to the destination you had planned for them.

There are options for detours with rocky roads.

There are options to drive into uncrossable ravines.

Other cars are speeding out of control.

There are even drunk drivers, going the wrong way.

Because of your love for your child, you are diligent to avoid all these things, taking only the best roads. You are willing to take that extra time to ensure safe travels, regardless of the complaints from your kiddo in the back seat nagging you to, "go faster", or them asking you, "how much longer?". In your eyes, it is worth the extra time to get your child to the planned destination safely, regardless of what they would prefer.

In essence, that is our relationship with Christ. He is the protective parent driving, and we are the nagging kid in the backseat.

Now imagine this.... Your child takes off their seatbelt, which is designed to protect them. They stand up, reach over you, and grab the wheel because they see something of interest to them coming up on an exit.

For the sake of this analogy let's say your kid saw a carnival because what kid doesn't get excited about carnivals? There are rides, games, lights, music, fun treats, and kettle corn. Man, that sounds exciting...

But that's not where you had intended to go. Especially because this particular carnival is in a bad part of town, and you have been there before. The people running the show are shady, the rides are falling apart, the food is expired, and the music is vulgar. You know that if you take your child there it's going to be in the best-case scenario risky, and downright dangerous in the worst.

Obviously, your child doesn't recognize any of that. All they see is the shiny lights, the music, and the rides, and are overwhelmed with their feelings of excitement and the thought of all the fun things that will come with it.

In essence that's us...

When the world comes calling, we don't stop to think about all the dangers that come from giving in to our fleshly desires. We only think about momentary satisfaction. We don't think about all the repercussions, consequences, and how our choices would affect others. We don't even think about how they would affect ourselves. Most importantly, we never stop to think about what God would want for us....

When the temptation of the world comes, we push Jesus out of the driver's seat, grab the wheel and jerk it in the direction we want to go!

SCREECH.......... CRASH!!!

That is when we crash into a wall head-on at full speed. Then we sit in the flaming pile of rubble and cry out to God.

GOD, WHY ME?!!!!

WHY THIS?!!!!

HOW COULD YOU LET THIS HAPPEN TO ME?!!!!

There are times we might even question His existence because of the train wreck our life has become as a result of our sin, or even worse, because of the sins of others....

He's got to be sitting there shaking His head looking at us thinking, "really?".

"I allowed you to choose, but I didn't tell you to choose it".

Or "that person's sin was their choice, not mine...."

Sometimes I feel like we are toddlers being told by our parents not to touch the hot stove a thousand times. Every time we reach out to touch it, He smacks our hand, or tells us "DON'T DO IT!". Eventually, He gets tired of warning us, and He allows us to touch the hypothetical stove. We creep up to it, look around, and think... OHHH, He's not looking, let me check out that thing He told me not to touch. We take our hand and smack it on the stove...

SMACK!

Just then we hear the sizzle, the heat strikes our nerves and causes us to screech out and pain. Tears well up and instantaneous regret overwhelm us.

He looks at us and says, "I told you not to touch the stove a thousand times.... Are you happy now?!!!!"

And we reply, "Why did you let me do that?!!!".

I think this is a very good reminder that we should bring all decisions before God in prayer. If He gives you an answer, listen!! The answer can come in all sorts of forms, it could be by the conviction of The Holy Spirit, through His Word, or maybe through another person.

But remember to always, always, always, weigh your answers against God's Word.

If the answer is contrary to scripture, we can know that it didn't come from the Lord. If after praying and waiting, you still haven't received an answer, go to the word, pray again, and ask again. You will get your answer eventually, remember He doesn't work according to our timing.

Sometimes His answer is yes, sometimes His answer is no, and sometimes His answer is not yet....

We need to learn patience and be willing to wait on God's timing because ultimately His timing is far better than ours.

I know it's hard to do.... Trust me, I know!!!

Especially because of my ADHD and the fact that we come from a society of instant gratification, but we must remember that God doesn't work that way. He is not a genie in a lamp, He is the creator of all things, the Lord God Almighty and He has a purpose and a plan for every one of us, according to His will and His timing. We need to stop jerking the steering wheel of our lives out of His hands and allow Him to drive.

Ok, great advice.... But how do we do that exactly?

We do that by walking in the wisdom of His word, by the strength and power of His Spirit, and with confidence in His faithfulness, and His love for us.

Maybe you're thinking, "That's great, but is there any biblical proof of what you're saying?". Let's take the story of Abraham and Sarah as an example.

God gave them the choice to follow Him and His promises or follow their desires. They felt God's timing was taking too long, so they started to think they misunderstood His directions. They decided God's promise to give Abraham a son, should have happened already, so they took matters into their own hands.

That is when they had a great idea!!

Abraham should sleep with his wife Sarah's servant Hagar, that way he could have a child through her.

Brilliant!!!

What could possibly go wrong?

They did this because Sarah previously was unable to have children, and since God promised Abraham a child, they figured maybe God meant for Abraham to have the child with Sarah's servant as a surrogate.

You know, maybe God just forgot to tell them that detail of His plan.

Obviously, we know that was not the case. And since we can read their story, we know how it ended.

This sexual union ended up bringing a child into the world whose name was Ishmael. That child ended up having animosity against Isaac who was the son promised by God. He was eventually born to Abraham by his wife Sarah.... (Huh, that's weird... Everything happened just like God said it would. Who would have thought that it all would have happened according to His timing, not theirs? It's almost like God's perfect timing is always better than ours because it is part of His ultimate purpose, and our impatience causes detours and stress in our life. Nah, must have just been a coincidence...)

We know that their impatience and choices caused animosity between Sarah and Hagar and ultimately forced Abraham to send away Hagar and his son Ishmael. Even though Abraham was impatient and disobedient, God still provided for Hagar and Ishmael. He even promised Ishmael to be a father of countless people, but with that promise also came a consequence for Abraham and his descendants through Isaac. Because Ishmael was promised to be a thorn in the side of his brother Isaac for all time.

There are so many times in our lives that we want God to act and move in the way that we expect Him to. And if He doesn't move as quickly as we expect, we force our decisions into our lives regardless of the answers we get from God.

Just like we saw in the story of Abraham and Sarah. They had the promise of Isaac, but by not understanding God's timing, they tried to force the outcome through their own will. And because of their impatience, God allowed them to stumble through their own choices. They had to experience the consequences of that decision, and unfortunately, Hagar and Ishmael also suffered because of the sins of others. But in God's perfect timing, He delivered the promised son Isaac. Just as He said He would because He is faithful and trustworthy (Genesis 21:1-2).

We can see very clearly how Abraham and Sarah's impatience and disobedience directly caused negative consequences for Hagar and Ishmael, not to mention the countless generations of both of their descendants that were also affected. This should be a stark warning and a reminder to us ALL that our sins affect people other than just us.

Do we ever stop and think that maybe, just maybe God takes His time because He knows exactly what we need when we need it?

Do we ever think that He is teaching us, patients, by testing our trust and our obedience? And through our impatience and disobedience, we are bringing more chaos and havoc to our own lives and the lives of others?

I think it's time that we all learn to be still and wait on God's perfect timing.

When He says to act, we should act.

When He says wait, we should wait.

and when He says NO, we need to realize that although we don't understand it, his purpose and reasoning are far better than our selfish desires.

Well.... We now have a very clear picture of why we should trust the Lord to drive, allow Him to handle the wheel, and why we need to keep our hands to ourselves.

Chapter 4

Jesus paid our debt... Let go of the Past!

Jesus paid our debt...
Let go of the Past!

It's so easy to get into the funk of beating ourselves up about the terrible things that we have done. Or maybe we are upset because lately, we have been stumbling in our walk with Christ. Or because we have been in an entire season of complacency, and we feel far from the Lord. Or maybe we are living in outright disobedience and are trying to find our way home.

That reminds me of the story of the prodigal Son seen in Luke 15:11-32. Most likely you've heard this story before, so I'm not going to beat it to death. But I do think that it is extremely important to take another look at it, but I'm just going to pick it up from the end. This is when the son had squandered his entire inheritance through "Reckless Living", which most likely means he spent it on women, partying, and debauchery. He finally found himself living in filth with the pigs and wishing that he could eat the slop they were eating. He realized that he had hit rock bottom...

He had to face reality and potentially had several choices.

First, he could have held onto his pride, and continued to live a life that was in disobedience to his father, a disgrace to his family, and ultimately continue in that pathetic excuse of an existence.

Well, he didn't want that. Especially since he was extremely unhappy with his current circumstances.

But to seek reconciliation with his father, he would have to swallow his pride and accept the fact that he made a ton of wrong choices.

We should stop here for a second and acknowledge that our **PRIDE** is an extremely dangerous thing. His pride could have kept him in the pit of hell that he was living in.

Another option he had was to give up and either allow himself to starve to death or take an even more selfish way out and end his own life.

This option is not something that anyone should consider, let alone follow through with. It would only be out of pure selfishness, or pride that would lead him to choose that decision.

Lastly, he could admit he was wrong, turn away from that lifestyle, and ask his father for forgiveness.

Clearly, this is by far the best option, and would only take a willingness to humble himself, admit fault, swallow his pride, and ask for forgiveness.

We can see in the story that the father was consistently looking for the return of his son. His heart was broken by his son's decisions and even though his son was disrespectful to him and his family, the father still missed and loved him.

We also see that when he was still a far way off, the father saw him and ran to him with open arms. This was showing that the father was not only actively looking for the return of his son but was also longing for the day that he would see him again.

One of my favorite parts of the story is the son's plan to give an entire speech to tell his father how sorry he was. He planned to explain how he was wrong and that he didn't even deserve to be his son anymore. The son was even willing to accept a position as one of his father's servants because he knew his disobedience was so hurtful. He just wanted a chance to live within the loving embrace of his father, even if it had to be as a servant because he knew that his father's servants were treated better than how he had treated himself.

Wow!!! That is powerful.

Just as the son opened his mouth to speak, the father interrupted him and didn't give him a chance. He ran to him, hugged him, put new clothes on him, put rings on his fingers, and threw a party in his son's honor.... All because his son had finally come home!

This is the story of us... It also explains clearly how God feels about us. How he wants us to return to Him and is actively looking for us and is waiting in anticipation of our repentance.

This should remind us who have repented and accepted His forgiveness, that although we were far from Him, we are home now.

Although we disrespected Him, He is happy that we have returned.

Although we have squandered what He had given us, He forgives us for our transgressions, He sees the repentance of our hearts and welcomes us home with a warm embrace.

When God looks at us now, He does not see us in the filthy garments that we once wore... Instead, He sees us covered in Christ's righteousness (2 Corinthians 5:21).

We have been forgiven by the blood of Christ, we are washed with his righteousness, and we never again are looked at as the broken filthy sinner that we were. Because now when the father looks upon us, He sees His Son's righteousness (1 Corinthians 1:28).

So, we should never let the enemy lie to us and tell us that we are not loved, or we are not good enough. We can never let him tell us that we are too broken, that we are too awful, that we are too wretched to be forgiven.

Don't ever let him tell us the lie that God remembers who we were, or that he sees us differently than other believers. The truth is all of humanity is wretched, broken, sinful, awful, disgustingly filthy, and putrid.... (If you are thinking this doesn't apply to you, maybe you should take a humble pill and recognize that compared to God's perfection we ALL fall short!) But God loved the world so much that he was willing to be born into His creation, to pay the debt of our sin with His blood so that we could be clothed in His righteousness.

So, whenever the father of lies (John 8:44) tries to tell us we are just broken sinners; we need to say, "Yes, I was a broken sinner, but I have been saved by the Grace of God, forgiven and covered by the blood of the Lamb (1 Peter 1:13-23).

Chapter 5

A New Creation

A New Creation

Now that we have taken the time to learn that we have been forgiven by the grace of God through faith in Jesus Christ alone (Ephesians 2:8). And that we are no longer remembered as sinners (2 Corinthians 5:21). We can move on to the next biblical understanding that we are no longer who we once were. Because we are now a new creation (2 Corinthians 5:17)!

Ok, what does that even mean?

I'll give you an analogy that can hopefully help you to understand.

Let's look at the process of a caterpillar turning into a butterfly. The caterpillar lives a life of complete selfishness, crawling around consuming and destroying everything within its path. It only has one thing on its mind and that is to satisfy its desire to consume. Day in and day out it wreaks havoc on everything around it.

In essence that's us before Salvation.

We were incapable of being selfless.

Selfishness consumed our every thought. Even things that looked to be selfless, had hidden ulterior motives. We consumed, we destroyed, and we wreaked havoc.

Obviously, the caterpillar was doing something that was going to bring benefit to it. The caterpillar needed to eat and build up its energy for its coming transformation.

But we were doing nothing that truly benefited us. We were only building up wrath for our judgment.

We can see this is where holes start to show up in this analogy, but hey, it's just a loose comparison....

Ok, back to what we were talking about. We had no benefit from our past, only destruction, and chaos. I know some of you who did not live as extreme of a life may look at what I'm saying and think to yourself, "man this guy is having fun exaggerating things!".

Let's get this straight.

Any sin is disobedience to God. God's standard is perfection. Anything outside of His perfection deserves death. So, whether we stole a piece of gum, or told a little white lie, we were being selfish, and wreaking havoc on ourselves. Because ultimately, we were all standing condemned for our disobedience (Romans 6:23). But thank God for His grace and His provision through the sacrifice of Jesus Christ!!

Now let's move to the next cycle. Before the transformation into a butterfly begins, the caterpillar must in a sense die to its old self. It crawls onto a branch and forms a chrysalis around itself, after some time passes, it emerges as something completely different than it was before.

It is now a butterfly.

It is no longer only capable of crawling, destroying, and wreaking havoc. It is now capable of flying to unimaginable heights and distances, its beauty and splendor are marveled at by others, and it brings inspiration and wonder to those who see it.

This is the stage in our analogy that represents our baptism. But by baptism, I mean the baptism of the Holy Spirit. This is when God called us into a state of repentance, and we listened to His call, repented, and accepted Him.

Remember when that overwhelming guilt for disobedience came upon you and was unshakable?

Or, when you first felt that desire to have something better in life?

You know...That first gravitation and pulling towards Christ that you could not explain, or even understand until you heard and accepted the Gospel.

That my friends was the call of the Holy Spirit!

And through your acceptance of the message of Jesus Christ, you were baptized and born again, by the power of the Holy Spirit. That is when we died to our old selves and became a new creation in Christ.

After this spiritual baptism, our life as believers changes drastically. I remember no longer having joy in the debauchery that I used to take so much pleasure in. If I was walking out of alignment with God, I felt guilt like I never had before. This is because we as believers have God's law written within us (Romans 2:12-16). The Holy Spirit is guiding us and redirecting us to the will of God if we stumble (John 16:13).

And on the other side of that equation, we now experience the fruit of the spirit; love, joy, peace, patience, kindness, goodness, faithfulness, gentleness, and self-control (Galatians 5:22-23), which we were incapable of experiencing before.

We are now capable of communicating with God through prayer and feeling a true connection to Him, His love, and His embrace. We are now able to open the scripture and through the power of the Holy Spirit, the words start to make sense. The truth of scripture is illuminated within our hearts.

I remember before I truly accepted Christ, I would try to read the Bible... And honestly, I had read quite a bit of it. But it never made any sense to me. I could read the words, but nothing clicked.

At that time, I felt like there was no power behind it. I never quite understood why... I didn't seem to get what others got from the Bible.

But after I was called by God, accepted Christ, and was baptized by the Holy Spirit, I was drawn to read scripture.

I opened my Bible, and my eyes were opened. My heart was softened, and the words spoke with Power and Truth.

I was able to understand things that I could never have wrapped my mind around before. The substance within the words called to my soul. I now had a hunger and an unquenchable thirst. I wanted to learn, study, and needed to know more (1 Corinthians 2:12-14).

I wanted to continuously talk about Jesus with others, I wanted to express this feeling that I couldn't explain. This is the rebirth and the explanation of being a new creation.

The major problem I ran into being an "on fire" new believer was that I did not surround myself with other "on fire" believers. I had stopped hanging out with most of my former friends, especially the ones who were involved in extensive criminal activities.

But some of the ones that were "okay", I stuck around with.

I would continuously talk to them about the transformation God did in my life. I would talk about Jesus and about the things I was learning from the Bible.

I was super excited and wasn't afraid to show it!

Some of them were open to listening, some of them didn't want to hear it, and others would throw water on my "fire".

They would say stuff like, "that's cool that God has done so much for you, but some of your understanding of what the Bible is saying is not right, because it was written in a different time.".

That really confused me.... I figured that since they were "Christians" longer than I was, they must know more than me....

I had so many lukewarm Christians telling me this stuff that I started to believe it. I even started to water down my understanding and interpretation of scripture. I started looking at the biblical accounts in a way where I would input my life, or modern society into God's Word to try to find the truth that fits.

That's what we Bible nerds call an eisegetical study, which I now understand is a completely wrong way to interpret God's Word.

What we are supposed to do is a type of study which is called exegesis. That is where we read the Bible within its specific context, we understand the meaning of the passages from the intended author to the specific audience. We also seek to understand their historical context, and the purpose of the writing to find the truth from within the context. Then we take that truth, extract it from the word and apply it to our life, regardless of if society thinks it's applicable or not.

Now that my friends is the proper way to interpret scripture and apply it to our lives.

Too many people are taught the opposite of that, they're taught to look at the Bible as an allegory, or good stories with moral nuggets.

That my friends is not the Truth!

ALL scripture, let me repeat that All Scripture is breathed out by God and profitable for teaching, for reproof, for correction, and training in righteousness (2 Timothy 3:16). We do not have the right to make scripture say what we want it to say.

We must bend ourselves to the Word of God, not force the Word of God to bend to us.

An easy way to remember this is, we bow before God, He does not bow before us!

Many of us who have lived such a broken life before our rebirth into Christ have a very difficult time when we have stirred up memories of our past.

It is not that we are positively remembering our past, but instead, we remember it with much regret and pain.

This is when the cracks in our lives start to show, and those are the cracks that Satan likes to dig his claws into. He takes advantage of these moments of weakness and tries to tear open and expose our old wounds. He creeps in with his lies and manipulation. He starts by telling us that we're not good enough, that Christ could never have forgiven us, that He doesn't love us, that we never were saved, or even worse that we "lost our salvation".

He tells us that we are too broken and too evil to be loved and used by God....

This is where I'm going to stop and make sure to clarify that this is a lie, birthed from the pit of Hell!

We know that Satan is the father of lies (John 8:44), he is the accuser of the brethren (Revelation 12:10), and his only job is to stop us as believers from being profitable to God and His purposes.

So of course, he wants to muddy our witness, make us ineffective, make us doubt ourselves, and even doubt our salvation.

Remember this, Satan wouldn't be attacking us if we were not a threat to his plans....

If we as Christians are walking outside of fellowship with strong believers, we are like a weak animal that has been separated from the herd. The Bible says that Satan prowls around like a roaring lion, seeking someone to devour (1 Peter 5:8).

That is why walking through life as a Christian alone is not only a bad idea, but it is not biblical.

We are commanded to stay in fellowship with other believers (Hebrews 10:25). We as believers are not each called the Body of Christ; we are ALL members of the body as a whole (1 Corinthians 12:12).

The body is what we call the invisible or Big "C" Church!

I know a lot of you may have been hurt by different Church institutions, specific denominations, and so on.

Welcome to the club!

But true Biblical Christianity is not religiosity or denominationalism. The Big "C" Church is the invisible Church of Christ. There is no denominational name slapped on it.

There is no such thing as my pastor said-so, so it's true.

Or, if you're not part of our group, your salvation does not count.

Or, I'm going to take one passage out of scripture and turn it into an entire theological doctrine and then parade myself around as some sort of circus freak telling other brothers and sisters that they are condemned....

Sorry, but that is heresy, and ridiculous and scripture speaks against these things. Paul tells us that we are not to separate the body of Christ (1 Corinthians 1:10-13). That passage is speaking boldly against denominationalism.

So, stop making excuses of why you won't join a Church and find yourself a solid Bible teaching Church.

Here is some advice; if somebody invites you to their Church, go to the Church's website, look at their profession of Faith, read through it, and if what they believe is not sitting well with you, or is not biblical, find a different Church to check out.

There are big Churches, medium Churches, Small Churches, home Churches, Churches that meet at coffee shops, and more.

None of us are exempt from the rule of fellowship, we are all part of the body, and we are needed for the Body to function properly. Not only are we needed, but we also need the support of the body as well. We guide each other, we correct each other, we love each other, we protect each other, we're here to help the hurt, and we're here to teach and sharpen each other.

I'm not going to promise you that it will not be messy at times since God designed us to work in unison with others. And because of that, we can sometimes cause each other hurt, frustration, and irritation. When situations like that happen, we need to remember to address those situations out of love, just like we would with our immediate "blood family". And if your immediate "blood family" happens to be ridiculous and dysfunctional, look at somebody else's family who is not, and use them as an example.

We as individual believers need to remember that each, and every one of us who make up the Church were all broken sinners, who are now covered by the blood of Christ, forgiven, and made new.

We also need to remember that our spiritual rebirth is spiritual, and if we are not walking by the guidance of the Holy Spirit and weighing our life in decisions against the word of God, our flesh will start to make decisions for us. We will see pride, arrogance, gossip, bickering, contentiousness, and more creep out of our lives and into the Body of Christ. If any of that putridness spews from within us onto our brothers and sisters, we need to have the humility to accept our faults, apologize and reconcile with them, immediately.

I'm not going to tell you that you will never make a mistake.

I can't promise you that you won't stumble.

I can't tell you that you'll be perfect.

Because unfortunately our flesh is still destined for death, and it is still hungry for sin even though The Holy Spirit in us is perfect (Romans 7:21-25).

We will feel that inner battle and turmoil amongst ourselves and we must not give in to our flesh. Because now we have someone fighting on our behalf (Romans 8:6-11). Before we had the indwelling of the Holy Spirit it was impossible for us to overcome our fleshly desires, but now it is possible (Galatians 5:16). We must continuously pray to our Father God to give us strength by the power of The Holy Spirit, so we can overcome trials and temptations.

Also, a continuous study of scripture and fellowship with strong believers will help sharpen and strengthen your walk. We experience this through progressive sanctification. That is the continued progress of the denial of our fleshly desires and replacing them with obedience to God's will by showing selflessness toward others. In essence, we need to pick up our cross and follow our Lord and Savior Jesus Christ. This is how we will grow as a believer into maturity.

We are called to deny ourselves from the things in life that do not bring glory to God. We can weigh that against the command that Jesus gave us. He told us that the two greatest commandments, that summarize the entirety of the Old Testament law, were this; First - love God with everything we have and put him first in our lives. And Second - we are called to love our neighbor as ourselves.

So ultimately after becoming a new creation, we need to put God first and live a selfless life of love, forgiveness, Grace, and generosity toward others. And don't worry if you feel like you're too broken for God to fix you. He'll pick up all the pieces, put them back together and you will no longer be able to see the cracks of your old life. Because He has covered ALL of them with the blood of Christ.

Chapter 6

Get in the Word

Get in the Word

We as believers hear the term "being in the word" thrown around quite often. It's a common phrase used regarding reading the Bible. Reading the Bible is one of the most important activities we as believers are to partake in. Without a deep-rooted understanding of God's word, how are we supposed to understand God's character, His promises, and how to follow Him properly?

Should we just listen to what others teach us about the Bible?

Ummmm NO!

The Bible was given to us to read and study (Deuteronomy 8:2-3, Matthew 4:4). The Bible tells us in 2 Timothy 3:16-17 All Scripture is breathed out by God and profitable for teaching, for reproof, for correction, and for training in righteousness, that the man of God may be complete, equipped for every good work.

Reading the Bible is the first step as a believer and a great way to get surface knowledge of God's word, and a basic understanding of the teachings of the Scripture. Through reading, we gain familiarity with the stories, teachings, and guidance that are essential to our Christian walk. But there is so much more to God's word than just reading. A deep study, meditation (deep thought about topics), and prayer are how we will grasp a greater understanding of Biblical truth.

Did you know that there are hundreds of thousands of cross-references interwoven throughout the Old, and the New Testaments?

We could spend an entire lifetime digging into scripture, reading every cross reference, diving into the historical context, and grasping a deep understanding of God's sovereignty and his divine purpose revealed through scripture, and still not get everything the Bible has to offer!

But that's only because God's word is not just any old book. The Bible was written over about 1500 years, by about 40 God-inspired individuals, as 66 individual books. But those books fit seamlessly together as one Great Book, that tells one amazing story. That story is of God's love for mankind, shown in the revealing of our Lord and Savior Jesus Christ.

We truly start to see God's absolute love for humanity, and the sacrifice He made for us through the work of Jesus Christ on the Cross. We can also see through the study of prophecy how God is in control of ALL things, both Big and Small while still allowing the Free Will of people. He can use the obedience, or disobedience of mankind for His plan, purpose, and outcome in the end. We will understand how far ALL of us truly are from His greatness. And we can start to realize how much we truly owe Him, and we will gain a greater understanding of how great and awesome God is.

By studying we will be more capable of listening to the guidance of the Holy Spirit because He will be able to direct us to the passages that we have studied in God's Word.

The Spirit will bring to light answers to questions when we need them. We will be able to guide others in their walk and our faith will be continuously strengthened and sharpened by His Word.

The constant in-depth study of God's Word is essential to our walk. And the fact that scripture is continuously quoted throughout the entirety of the Bible, shows its importance and necessity in our lives.

How many of us have Bibles laying around our house collecting dust?

I was listening to a pastor who was talking about his trip to China. He was saying how bibles are restricted over there and that so many pastors have been imprisoned for either teaching God's word, or just having possession of it. Because of this, they are constantly working to memorize scripture. They know that they will not always be able to have a physical copy and appreciate the importance of God's Word.

They hold the Bible as sacred and value it as Gold, just as it should be.

But here in America, we have an abundance of Bibles stacked a mile high collecting dust.

They are never being read.

And we take for granted the blessings we have.

Okay, my rant is over!

You may be saying to yourself, okay I see what you're saying but how exactly do you study the Bible beyond just reading it?

I'm glad you asked! It is important to study the Bible in depth. Reading it is great, but studying it brings a deep understanding and practical ability to implement the truth and teachings into our lives.

The proper way to study the Bible is called historical, hermeneutical exegesis. This is where we find the truth within the context of what the writer was saying to the audience, within the understanding of their circumstances and culture. We then extract that truth and apply it to our lives.

Unfortunately, many people fall victim to a misinterpretation of scripture by using a different style of interpretation called eisegesis. That is where we would implant our life, modern society, or current social understandings into the Bible to try to find the truth that fits what we are looking for. This will lead to massive misinterpretations and misrepresentations of the truth within the Bible.

It would be like taking a conversation that two individuals had and removing the context and isolating a small fraction of that conversation while inserting ourselves into the scenario and conversation and using it to make a point.

Imagine two people having a 2-hour conversation about their life, their relationships, and their concerns. One of them is specifically advising another about an area in life that they are struggling in. Now part of that conversation is specifically about behavior that they're struggling with. They know it's wrong, but they enjoy doing it, so they are having a hard time stopping it.

For example, one of the people says, "I like partying and getting high, but I know it's wrong. I feel so bad and am feeling convicted for doing it. I want to walk away from that behavior... I can no longer live in sin; I've asked God for help and am moving into obedience to Him."

The other person responds, "I completely understand what you're going through and agree with your conclusion. That behavior may be enticing, but it is not worth going against what God wants for your life and it will dig you into a hole of unhappiness, depression, and despair! I will be praying for you to have wisdom and strength and I'm here for you if you need anything."

Now.... What if someone else came along and read that conversation and only took bits and pieces out of it to make a point for themselves?

They could take out, "I enjoy partying and getting high" from one person and "I completely understand what you're going through and agree" from the other, put them together, and bring an entirely different meaning to the conversation.

Unfortunately, that happens way too often with the Bible. That's why context, historical background, understanding the writer and the audience, and the genre that it was written in, is so important to interpreting and studying the Bible properly. I've included a list of ways to study and interpret the Bible properly for reference.

Here are some keys to Bible interpretation:

The Golden rule of grammatical and historical biblical hermeneutics. If the plain sense of the text makes common sense, seek no other sense.

Note When dealing with prophecy, it is important to understand that we must let the Bible clarify what symbols and signs are intended to mean. First look within the immediate context, to see if it reveals the answer. If it is not revealed in the immediate context of that passage, look in that same book, by checking that chapter and the following chapters. If you still have no clarity, then check the passages you have already read that are behind that passage. You can also see if the signs and symbols are explained anywhere else in the Bible. We must never just make it up as we go. Also, while dealing with prophecy, we have a biblical understanding that prophetic statements will often have a dual fulfillment. The first "partial fulfillment" is a picture or a type of the ultimate fulfillment, and the ultimate would take place at a later date. The initial partial fulfillment was to give assurance to the immediate audience that the later fulfillment would be fulfilled and the prophecy could be trusted, and that it truly came from God.

Who wrote the Book or Letter?

Who was the Audience?

What was the Historical background and culture of the people being addressed?

Why was the Book or Letter written?

What issues were being addressed in the letter or book?

What Genre was the Book or Letter written in? (Poetry, Historical, Apocalyptic, Letter, etc....)

What does the Entirety of that Book or Letter say about the topics as a whole? Do not cherry-pick or read passages or sentences out of Context!

Did the author write other Books or Letters to the same People? If so, cross reference topics in question or difficult verses.

Did the author write other Books or Letters to other people to reference similar topics or phrases, or terminology being used? If so, cross reference topics in question or difficult verses.

What does the rest of Scripture say about those same topics?

What do the cross-reference or parallel passages in scripture say to clear up any misunderstanding or confusion?

We must always use the Bible to interpret the Bible. Not conjecture or presupposition.

NOTE - Listening to commentary on difficult passages is helpful, but DO NOT base your whole understanding of the bible on the opinions of others. Put in the work and do your own research to ensure you are getting good information.

It's great if they back up their conclusion with scripture, but we still need to read, or listen to multiple commentaries and ALWAYS check everything they are saying with the scripture itself.

Be careful some commentators will pull supporting passages they are using for arguments that are taken out of context to support their ideas or argument.)

I recommend using Bible Gateway or Logos, and the Blue Letter Bible app (which is Good for cross-referencing the original language it was written in, by its interlinear function, which is connected to the Strong's Concordance.). I use the LSB translation because it adheres to word-for-word literal translation and its readability and accuracy. The LSB is the updated version of the NASB1995. I like to jump between translations for more difficult passages, in conjunction with the concordance to get a clearer understanding of the original text. I also recommend that you get a study bible with a concordance, maps, and historical intro-ductions. They are very helpful! Now you are ready to dig into God's word!

***Please know that I am in no way affiliated with any translation, company, or phone app. I am just giving my opinion and giving you the tools that I use.

Chapter 7

Walk the Walk

Walk the Walk!

Over the years I've had to look at myself clearly during my walk with Jesus. When I first received the baptism of the Holy Spirit I was on fire for the Lord and my life was completely transformed. He called me out of a life of sexual immorality, violence, crime, debauchery, drugs, and a love for my sin.

I tried to walk the Christian walk alone and was slowly beaten down by my flesh, my worldly desires, and lukewarm believers, which allowed my life to look less and less like Christ.

There was eventually a slight restoration away from complacency and an inching toward rejuvenation as I found fellowship with other believers.

But I didn't fully commit to building relationships with my brothers and sisters in Christ. I tried to walk a line between what I wanted and what God wanted for me.

As the years progressed, I realized more and more how far I walked away from God's purpose for me. Even though at that time they were very small steps, over a long period they took me so far off course I almost didn't know where I was.

It's like a ship whose navigator is off 1°, in a short period it's not noticeable. But when traveling across the ocean, you manage to end up in an entirely different destination.

Looking back, I can see how God has used so much of what has happened in the world lately to call me back into alignment, strengthen me and reroute me in His Word.

The change He is making and has made in my life is not only noticeable, but my old self is becoming more and more unrecognizable. I have left complacency behind and am serving the Lord with my mind, heart, soul, and strength.

Without the guidance and direction of God in my life, I would not be where I am today. I'm so grateful for His patience, His grace, and His blessings on me and my family. God did not only save my physical life the night He called me into repentance, but the Lord also protected me from the path of destruction I had chosen for myself. He most importantly saved my soul from the eternity of separation from Him in darkness, torment, and anguish.

I'm being honest with you about my struggles within my walk with Christ to hopefully encourage you.

We must remember that none of us are perfect, but God is!

He is capable and He is willing to help us through our times of need.

All He asks is that we submit to Him and listen to His guidance.

As Christians, we need to remember that the world sees our behavior, more than they listen to our words. So, we need to make sure our behavior speaks the same message that we are preaching. We as believers are the light of the world, and as the Body of Christ, we should not be hiding in our holy huddles. We need to let our light shine before others, so that they may see our good works and give glory to our Father who is in heaven (Matthew 5:14-16). And even though at one time we were darkness, now we are light in the Lord, so we must walk as children of light (Ephesians 5:8-10).

It is very easy in this current age to get distracted.

It's easy to compromise our witness and live a life of conformity and complacency.

But we are called not to conform to this world, but rather to live in obedience to God through our words, actions, and lives (Romans 12:1-2). Because God prefers obedience over sacrifice (1 Samuel 15:22). So, I pray that God gives us All the strength we need to be the ambassadors He called us to be.

We know that the Bible shows clearly that Jesus loves the ones that society rejected and considered unlovable. He preached repentance and forgave the broken who were willing to have enough humility to trust in the promises of God and turn away from their sinful ways. The Bible also says that Christ willingly died for us when we were still his enemies (Romans 5:10). He rose from the Dead to show us that He is the only Way, the only Truth, and the only Life (John 14:6) and that if we have seen Him then we have seen the Father (John 14:8-10) since He and the Father are One (John 10:10). We are also told that if anyone preaches a Gospel other than that; whether it be an "Angel", or a man let them be "damned" (Galatians 1:8-9).

So, if we want to know what Jesus would want us to do, it's this; Preach to the world about the sacrifice and forgiveness that He offers by the grace of God the Father. Explain how we are separated from God because of our sinful nature. And how we had no hope to repay the debt we owed Him. So, God willingly came down and was born in human form to pay a price for all of humanity.

Because He knew that no one could pay that debt for themselves. After His death on the cross, He rose from the dead. Making Him the firstborn from death to the resurrection (Colossians 1:18). By doing so He now offers equal opportunity to all people to be saved. This offer is accessible regardless of race, socioeconomic status, language, education, or societal acceptance. We all can now be forgiven through His blood, and reunited with God by His grace, through faith in Jesus Christ and His promises.

We as believers must now show love to those who are still broken, help those who are in need, and remind those who are self-righteous, that it is not by any doing of our own that we have been saved. We are only saved by the grace of God through faith in Jesus Christ alone, so none of us can boast in our salvation. And finally, we must not forget about Jesus telling us the importance of turning away from our sins, sacrificing our sinful desires, picking up our cross, and following Him.

Now we can see that by preaching the Gospel to the broken world and showing selfless love for the people we encounter daily, out of gratitude for what God has given to us, is how we walk the walk.

Chapter 8

Throwing Seeds

Throwing Seeds

The word "Gospel" is a term used in Christianity very often, and we as Christians are called to Share that "Gospel", but what does that even mean?

Well, the word itself means "Good News".

So, Christians are called to share the Good News! All right I am glad we cleared that up. Have a great day!

Okay, Okay.... I am just kidding; we obviously must elaborate a little more than a literal definition of the word itself.

So, what does The Good news mean from a Biblical Christian perspective?

Well, the Bible teaches that we as people have ALL "sinned" (Fallen short of the perfection of God Romans 3:23). The Bible says that when we break even one law, we have broken them ALL (James 2:10). The Bible also teaches that the wages of SIN are DEATH (Romans 6:23) ...

Soooo there's that!!!

We also know through The Bible's teaching that God is Righteous, Just, and Holy. He promised that ALL Sin would be punished by the DEATH of our physical bodies first, and then the second death which is eternal separation from His presence.

Hey, that doesn't sound too bad....

It's in a place of eternal torment and pain!!!

Ummmm....NO THANKS!

Well, thankfully the Bible also tells us that God's Love for us was so great that He wanted to forgive us and offer an opportunity for redemption to us ALL.

But, since He promised that sin would be punished, and He can't take back His promises, He chose to show the greatest expression of LOVE the universe has ever known.

He came down from heaven, and entered His creation being born as Jesus Christ (Colossians 1:16). Although He was fully man, He was also still Fully God, and though PERFECT and BLAMELESS He willingly died on the Cross, to cover the debt of OUR SIN that we could never have paid, and 3 days later He resurrected Himself from the dead.

By His actions, He conquered both SIN and DEATH once and for ALL (1 Peter 3:18).

We now have the opportunity of "SALVATION" (acceptance into God's presence and presented to Him as perfect by the finished work of Jesus Christ, not of any work of our own) by the "Grace" (unmerited favor) of God, Through Faith in the promise of salvation that Jesus Christ offered to us ALL through HIS sacrifice.

So how do we accept this Gift?

We need to first recognize that we have ALL sinned and have fallen short of God's Perfection, confess our sins, and "repent" (Turn away from disobedience to His word). Truly Believe in our heart and confess with our mouth that Jesus is our Lord and Savior, that He is the Christ, the Son of the Living God.

We are to recognize that He conquered Sin by His Death on the Cross, which paid the payment for our sin that we couldn't pay on our own, because of our corrupted sinful nature.

He then conquered death by His resurrection into eternal Life, and He is now seated at the right hand of the Father.

Now finally we are commanded to be Baptized in the name of the Father, Son, and The Holy Spirit.

This represents our death to our old life in bondage to sin, and a rebirth as a new creation into the family of God. Water baptism is an outward expression of the inward work God has done inside of us through the baptism of the Holy Spirit, through the finished work of Jesus Christ.

Ephesians 2 tells us that we are saved by the grace of God, through faith in Jesus Christ, not by any works of our own so nobody can boast, since it was not by our "good" works that we were saved. We are told that it is a gift from God, accomplished by the perfect work and sacrifice of Jesus Christ!!

Using our testimony, and our experiences with God's grace, and by building trust and relationships with others is a wonderful way to open the door to the Gospel.

We can't drag our feet in doing this.

We also shouldn't think, somebody else will share Jesus with them.

We are commanded as believers to spread the Good News.

Let's take a look at the parable of the Sower, to see how that is done.

The Parable of the Sower - Matthew 13:1-23 That same day Jesus went out of the house and sat beside the sea. And great crowds gathered about him so that he got into a boat and sat down. And the whole crowd stood on the beach. And he told them many things in parables, saying: "A sower went out to sow. And as he sowed, some seeds fell along the path, and the birds came and devoured them. Other seeds fell on rocky ground, where they did not have much soil, and immediately they sprang up, since they had no depth of soil, but when the sun rose they were scorched. And since they had no root, they withered away. Other seeds fell among thorns, and the thorns grew up and choked them. Other seeds fell on good soil and produced grain, some a hundredfold, some sixty, some thirty. He who has ears, let him hear." Then the disciples came and said to him, "Why do you speak to them in parables?" And he answered them, "To you it has been given to know the secrets of the kingdom of heaven, but to them it has not been given. For to the one who has, more will be given, and he will have an abundance, but from the one who has not, even what he has will be taken away. This is why I speak to them in parables, because seeing they do not see, and hearing they do not hear, nor do they understand. Indeed, in their case the prophecy of Isaiah is fulfilled that says: """You will indeed hear but never understand, and you will indeed see but never perceive." For this people's heart has grown dull, and with their ears they can barely hear, and their eyes they have closed, lest they should see with their eyes and hear with their ears and understand with their heart and turn, and I would heal them.' But blessed are your eyes, for they see, and your ears, for they hear. For truly, I say to you, many prophets and righteous people longed to see what you see, and did not see it, and to hear what you hear, and did not hear it. "Hear then the parable of the sower: When anyone hears the word of the kingdom and does not understand it, the evil one comes and snatches away what has been sown in his heart. This is what was sown along the path. As for what was sown on rocky ground, this is the one who hears the word and immediately receives it with joy, yet he has no root in himself, but endures for a while, and when tribulation or persecution arises on account of the word, immediately he falls away. As for what was sown among thorns, this is the one who hears the word, but the cares of the world and the deceitfulness of riches choke the word, and it proves unfruitful. As for what was sown on good soil, this is the one who hears the word and understands it. He indeed bears fruit and yields, in one case a hundredfold, in another sixty, and in another thirty."

Here is an explanation of that parable. The first two seeds sown in this parable are shown to be unbelievers, it's very apparent by the explanation Jesus gives.

The last two are the ones that most people stumble upon. Believe it or not, the last one is the only believer.

One of them, the one that is choked by the weeds, refers to a Nominal Christian living a carnal, or fleshly life that is unfruitful. John 15 clearly shows that only those who abide in Christ can bear fruit. and since the third seed never bore fruit we can see they are unbelievers.

The final seed is a believer who is living a life in the spirit producing fruit and being a good ambassador for Christ. A good representation of this type of believer would be found in the book of Revelation, in the letter to the Church of Philadelphia and 3 John to Gaius (Revelation 3:7-13, 3 John 1:1-4).

To the carnal or flesh-driven Nominal Christian, a warning should be made. Test yourself to see if you are in Christ! (2 Corinthians 13:5)

We as believers will face Christ at the bema seat, which is the Judgment for the believer. He will judge our works both good and bad and our eternal reward will be based on our faithfulness and obedience and our use of the time, talents, and treasures He has given us (1 Corinthians 3:15).

But let me clarify... That judgment is not regarding our salvation. Our works as a result of our salvation are what is being judged at the Bema seat.

And we know through scripture that we are not saved through our works, but only by the grace of God, through faith in the finished works that Christ Himself did on the Cross on our behalf. But because of that saving faith, we will have good works as a result and have an opportunity to be rewarded for those good works.

What can we figure out now that we have more information about this parable?

Well, we know that the Sower is throwing seeds indiscriminately. He's not too concerned with where he's throwing the seed, he's just throwing it at every place he encounters.

What do we know about him?

He represents Christ (Matthew 13:37), and we are called to be ambassadors for Christ (2 Corinthians 5:20).

The seed is the Word of God, or more specifically the Gospel, and the soil that the seed falls on represents the different conditions of the heart.

Some hearts are hardened like a hard path and the seed cannot penetrate through the hardness of that heart.

Some of the soil is Rocky showing that the heart is only partially hardened. The word of God will sprout up there, but because of the partial hardening, it cannot take root within the heart and gets burned up.

The other soil shows that the heart is not hardened, but it also has weeds. These are the worries and love for the world and what it offers. These things choke out the nutrition from the "plant". Not killing it but making it so it does not produce fruit.

That is showing us that this Nominal Christian has never fully placed their faith in Christ, because of their love for the world.

Finally, the last soil represents the heart that is fully open to the Gospel. That heart allows roots to grow and as it is being cultivated (Sanctified) it releases its love and worries for the world, which allows it to produce fruit for the kingdom. Showing that this believer has reached maturity and will be spreading the Gospel on behalf of the Kingdom of God.

What have we learned?

The Sower goes out and spreads seeds indiscriminately everywhere!

From the outside, we look at the sower, and we're thinking... "Man, is he ever going to run out of seeds? He's throwing them all over the place and not even caring where they go!"

Well, that is the intent of the parable. We as Ambassadors for Christ have an infinite number of opportunities to spread the Gospel. It is not up to us whom we share with. Every single person is eligible to hear the Gospel, no matter where they are in life.

You would think that coming from an understanding of my past debauchery and brokenness, I wouldn't need to be reminded of this...

Well, you'd be wrong!

I have failed at spreading the Gospel to people so many times, just because I looked at their lives and thought to myself how could they ever want to hear what I'm going to tell them?

What!?

I know... That is so ridiculous! It's like the Apostle Paul said, "how are they to believe if no one tells them (Romans 10:14-17)?".

What we all need to remember is, we are not the ones responsible for the growth of the seed! We are only responsible for planting them and watering them. Planting them is spreading the Gospel. If the Gospel is received, then we are to water that seed, by guiding them and teaching them from the Bible. We can also help them to find a Church that will guide them on the path to maturity. But the growth comes from God alone, and scripture backs that up (1 Corinthians 3:6-7).

Whew... That takes ALL the pressure off!!

It is not our responsibility to make them believe...

Let me repeat that, it's not our responsibility to make them believe.

It's only our responsibility to shine the light on the Truth of the Gospel.

I like to think of evangelizing in this way. If we had a cure for the deadliest disease on the planet, and everyone caught it, would we share that cure with everybody that we know?

If the answer is yes and if we are professing Christians, we have that cure!

The disease that infects the entirety of the world is sin, depravity, and most of all unbelief. And the only cure for that disease that they are dying from is the Gospel.

The Gospel of Jesus Christ shows the brokenness of every human being, it reveals God's love for us, and Jesus's willingness to die for us. It explains how He paid for our sins, while we were still His enemies, and through His blood, we can be cured of eternal death.

He paid the debt that we could not, so we could obtain salvation through him, which we could have never done on our own!

We also must remember while interacting with unbelievers that we should never be trying to correct the world's sinful behavior, one behavior at a time.

This would be foolishness on our part.

Because we know behavior modification is NOT the path to Salvation.

It is only through the grace of God by faith in Jesus Christ alone that leads to Salvation. And by that salvation, we are born again spiritually, the Holy Spirit lives within us and shows us Truth. And by that Truth, our behavior begins to change through our progressive sanctification.

So, let's go out and spread the Gospel, not out of condemnation, judgment, or fear. But instead, out of love for those who are lost, and because of our gratitude to God for what He has forgiven us for.

Remember we were all broken sinners before we were covered by the grace of God through faith in Christ. We did not obtain anything by our own doing, so none of us have the right to boast in righteousness since it is not our own. We are only to boast in the righteousness of God and His grace that he bestowed on us through our faith in the Lord Jesus Christ.

So instead of casting judgment, we need to have empathy. And instead of condemnation, we need to keep throwing the seeds of the Gospel. Don't misunderstand, we must always expose sin, but we must give the Gospel as the solution.

I use my past and testimony to expose sin, and preach the Gospel to others. I have found that exposing sin by pointing to my faults helps people to be more receptive.

Chapter 9

Jesus doesn't need us; He Wants us!

Jesus doesn't need us; He Wants us!

We need to stop listening when the enemy whispers into our ears and tells us we're not good enough. He will consistently sell us lies if we keep buying them. We believe that we could never contribute to the body of Christ. We think we are too broken, we're not good enough, and we've made too many mistakes.

We have also seen people on the other side of that mindset thinking that they are God's gift to humanity. They act like without their single-handed self-righteousness, the kingdom could never be established.

Obviously, we can see that both are extreme cases, and both are ridiculous.

The reason God set up His Church the way that He did was not that He needed us to do anything for Him. Let's be honest, we couldn't even do anything for ourselves!

He was showing us through His example of selflessness how we are to act towards each other. And knowing our tendencies to work alone, He decided to force us to work together.

We are supposed to be loving, gracious, kind, forgiving, selfless, and helpful to others. And the Church body is supposed to work in harmony as one single unit. Everyone provides a service through the God-given spiritual gifts that are obtained by God's will through the power of the Holy Spirit. And each member works in unison and harmony with one another to help the body to function properly.

It doesn't take too much mental gymnastics to figure out why He called it the body of Christ. It was to give us a wonderful analogy to wrap our minds around. And since we each have a physical body, that helps us to understand how the body (Church) is supposed to function.

Each part no matter how important plays an intricate role within the body, some parts you don't even think about, but without them, the body couldn't function.

It's so we can't ever look at ourselves as being less than others because our spiritual gift may not be as important as theirs.

To the body, your gift is essential and of the utmost importance. I bet you don't think your pinky toe is very important until it gets chopped off and you lose balance and have trouble walking.

In the same way, maybe the person who serves in the preschool at the church doesn't seem important until they're not there to do it.

Or maybe the person who sets up the chairs doesn't seem important until there's nowhere to sit.

Maybe the person who greets others at the door doesn't seem important until people walk in and feel unwelcome.

We seem to put so much emphasis on the "higher" gifts and forget that all gifts are given to us by God. They were not given to us to divide us; they were given to us to benefit the body as a whole and for us to work together as a team. We should all be thankful for the gifts that we were given and use them to glorify God. We should never look down on others because their gifts are "less important". We should be going out of our way to appreciate those who are using their gifts, whether big or small to glorify God.

He does not need us to have our life together before he is willing to offer us forgiveness.

He just needs us to be willing to follow Him, and He takes care of the rest.

Remember, we are ALL saved by the grace of God through faith in Jesus Christ, we are sealed with the Holy Spirit as a guarantee of our salvation. Also, we are each gifted to serve one another selflessly, out of reverence and worship to our heavenly Father.

Jesus doesn't ask for our qualifications before He calls us into service. Because He doesn't call the equipped, He equips the Called! This is clearly showing us that Jesus doesn't need us; He wants us!

Chapter 10

Gather, Grow, Serve, Repeat!

Gather, Grow, Serve, Repeat!

I'm not sure how it is in the rest of the world when it comes to this, but I know here in America we have a huge problem with consumerism when it comes to the Church. We feel like the Church was created to serve us, the sermons need to be to our liking, the music needs to be to our taste, and other people better be doing their best to make sure that we're comfortable. We show up when we want, we do not want to be inconvenienced and the minute we become unhappy we either throw a temper tantrum or find a new church. The plague of consumerism is turning the Church into a broken home. We were not called to be consumers; we were called to be servants to one another.

Have we forgotten that everything we have is given to us by God?

I think there are times we need to step back and remember how much God has done for us. Every single one of us deserves eternal damnation for our disobedience, but instead, we were offered forgiveness and salvation.

Was Christ willing to suffer and die on our behalf, so we could continue to be selfish, not care about each other and expect to be served by others?

Or did He save us from ourselves by His selflessness so that we could become selfless and serve others?

The reason He has given us the time, talents, and treasures that we have is to use them in a way that would bring glory to Him.

How much time do we spend streaming videos, arguing on social media, binging shows, talking politics and nonsense, and so on?

Is that time well spent?

Do we spend most of our God-given time for selfish purposes?

We should stop and consider a better way to spend the gift of time that we have.

How about our talents, how are we using those? Are we using them to benefit our local Church, Christian nonprofit organizations, evangelizing, or serving others selflessly?

These talents were given to us for a purpose, as part of the body of Christ each of us is to fill a role in service to the body. Whether our talents are small or great, they can be used and utilized for the benefit of spreading the Gospel. So, we need to take the time to recognize what our talents and giftings are. Then we need to find out how God wants to use those talents and giftings to bring glory to

His name, to spread His Gospel to the broken world, and to shine His light in these dark times.

Ok, now we come to the most controversial part.... What about our money? Are we using our finances to buy the nicest and best things for ourselves, or are we using them to help those who are less fortunate, fund Ministry work, and benefit the body of Christ?

Now don't get me wrong, if God has blessed you with financial success, there's nothing wrong with spending some of your money to live comfortably.

But showing generosity and having a heart for others is more important than having an abundance.

We are told that we are to build our treasures in Heaven where thieves, rust, and moth will not destroy them.

So, my warning to us all is to watch our hearts when it comes to our money because we know that the love of money is the root of all evil.

By now you might be thinking to yourself what the heck happened to this guy? I thought this book was about Never being too Broken for God....

Where are all the fluffy, make-you-feel-good messages and preaching?

Sorry, no fluff from me...

But never being too Broken for God is exactly what this book is about. You have seen that I was a broken piece of garbage who chose to live a selfish life, and how God called me and is using me for His Glory.

God called us out of the pit of hell so He could use us to preach to other broken people.

He doesn't want us to stay lukewarm and complacent, He wants us to live by example, to walk in a way that brings glory to Him. We are to give testimony not through just our words, but also through our lives because we were called to be ambassadors for Christ.

I know how much He has saved me from, so that's the least I can do for Him!

Would you rather I preach a watered-down version of the Gospel and tell you that God wants you to be happy and live your best life?

That's pretty much the same garbage that we were living with before we came to Christ; the only difference is that we would be trying to add God into that mix. Our temporal lives are not the end game, the end game is eternity.

We were called to see the world differently. Our eyes should be set on eternity, not on this world. We were called according to God's purposes, not our wants or our selfish desires.

His Kingdom draws near, the world is broken and needs Truth. We need to stand firm in biblical Truth, preaching the Gospel to those we encounter and spending our time, talents, and treasure in a way that will benefit the kingdom and bring glory to God.

Now that we have taken the time to run through all that, we have a firm understanding of what we are called to do. I would recommend looking at your schedule in your budget to see where you stand.

I did that myself a couple of years ago and was shocked at how much time I wasted, how much money I blew, and how little effort I put into proclaiming the Kingdom.

We all need to take a hard look at ourselves and remember whom we serve and why, and use that as motivation to Gather, Grow and Serve in the body of Christ.

Chapter 11

Why is the world broken?

Why is the world Broken?

Why is the world so broken? That is a philosophical question that people have tried to answer throughout time. The Bible offers us an answer. Sin... That is literally it! God set up a perfect world that was balanced with peace, unity, and love. He allowed mankind to have free will, and only set one rule. That one rule was laid out in the book of Genesis chapter 3, do not eat from the tree of the knowledge of Good and evil. The moment that man and woman decided to disobey God was the moment that sin was introduced into the world.

How could eating the fruit from a tree cause the destruction that we see today? That doesn't make any sense!

Well, I'm glad you asked, and I'll be happy to explain that to you.

The fruit was not the real issue, it was the fact that they disobeyed God. His setting only one rule wasn't a test for Him to see if mankind would fail. Remember God is sovereign He knows all things. It was to show us that even with one simple rule, we could never obtain righteousness on our own.

That one act of disobedience brought forth all the destruction and calamity that we see today. God had promised Adam that if they ate from that tree, they would have to face death, both physical and spiritual. After reading Genesis 3 we can see that because of Adam and Eve's disobedience, God had to kill an animal to clothe them, which was covering their shame (sin). This was the first symbolic gesture of an atoning sacrifice. That ultimately pictured that God would sacrifice the blood of an innocent to cover the sins of all. Just like the scripture says, we are clothed in Christ's righteousness, and we are covered by His blood.

The Bible says that even before God created us, He planned to save us from ourselves because He knew that we would disobey Him. Because of their sin, God cursed the land. Since Adam was formed from the earth, he too was cursed as a result. And we know that Eve had to endure the curse as well because she was formed from Adam.

We can see that the curse was passed on from the earth to Adam, to woman. Therefore, throughout time, the curse is passed through the seed (sperm) of man, to the children of women. This shows how Christ's virgin birth, through the power of the Holy Spirit allowed him to be born without the sin of Adam being passed on to Him.

Now let's go back one more step, to find out why Adam and Eve decided to disobey God in the first place.

That is an easy one.... Satan!

He slithered his way in, and whispered lies to Eve, enticing her curiosity, by bringing up questions and doubts about God's motives, His truthfulness, and His faithfulness.

Satan was able to get Eve to doubt God which stirred up pride within her. That resulted in her wanting to eat from the tree, not because the fruit looked better than the rest of the garden, but because of what Satan said.

He said that it would make her and Adam like God because they would know the difference between Good and evil.

This understanding was restricted from our mental capacities to protect us. Without the knowledge of good and evil, we could not act in sinful ways. But now with this knowledge, we not only sin, but we passed that inherited sinful nature down to countless generations. Sin wreaks havoc on our society, leaving us in a broken terrible mess of a world.

We know that the consequence of sin is death. On top of that, we know that there are so many more consequences that are immediate and prominent within the world today. Every time we commit a sin it has a consequence, not only in our lives but also in the life of those who are around us.

Many of us have been the cause of hurt, devastation, destruction, and pain toward those whom we encounter. This is all because of our sinful nature, and terrible choices.

There are so many who suffer at the hands of others and their sin. They are the ones whom I would like to address. This is an extremely difficult topic, and it is very sensitive.

The question that is often asked is, "if God is above all things, is capable of all things, and knows all things, why does he allow such terrible things to happen?" You have seen me address the topic of God's perfect love and sovereignty throughout the entirety of this book. But I would like to break that down into a deeper understanding. I felt this was very important because this topic causes so much confusion which results in pain, and resentment directed at God.

Yes, God does know all.

And Yes, He is capable of all things.

But we need to remember that God gave us free will. And it is our choices or the choices of others that bring pain and devastation to this world through sin.

The sinful behaviors of those who harm children, abuse their spouses, rob, murder, rape and so much more, not only have a negative and detrimental effect on that individual and their eternal life, but also on the victims of whom they have perpetrated these horrendous acts against and on all of society.

We need to understand that since God has given us free will, He can't go around stopping every atrocity that happens.

Not because He doesn't have the power to.

But because it would ultimately negate the free will which He bestowed upon us. Which would cause His Word to be untrue, and His actions would declare himself a liar....

Well, we know that scripture says that God can't lie and that He is the Word of Truth.

So, this is obviously not a plausible option.

Another option would have been to not create mankind at all.

God foreknew the devastation that we would bring upon creation. He knew of our disobedience and evil, and that we would revolt against Him. He also knew the pain and anguish that the world would face because of our sinful desires and our leanings toward disobedience.

But He also knew the joy, the love, the happiness, the laughter, the family gatherings, and the beauty that we would bring. He saw the light through our potential for darkness.

He had such a great love for us as His creation, even before He created us. And since He wanted to experience an opportunity to have a relationship with us, He decided to create us, even though He had the foreknowledge of how far we would fall.

He knew that by offering us free will, we would need redemption.

He knew the only path to that redemption would be through a perfect sacrifice.

And since He knew nothing within His creation would be able to achieve that perfect sacrifice, He decided that

He would personally redeem us through His Blood on the Cross.

His willingness to suffer and die for our disobedience shows the greatest example of selfless love that the Universe has ever seen. It paints a picture of understanding for us, that we can look back to when we are in times of hurt, especially at the hands of others.

Because through His love and redemption, we know that this life, although broken, has a greater purpose. That purpose is the rebirth of creation into eternal life. It is there where we will no longer experience sickness, hurt, pain, and death. We will no longer live in disobedience and rebellion and will be freed from the curse of sin in the world.

Through the redemption of Jesus Christ, we now can enter the paradise that God had intended for us before creation began. We can now experience His goodness in full measure in the eternal Kingdom. The hope that is offered to us, is not the temporal joy and peace that we experience in this world. It is the eternal joy, peace, and happiness that we need to fix our eyes upon, knowing that the brokenness of this world has an end.

Hopefully, that gives a deeper understanding of the origin of brokenness in this world. We must always remember to focus our frustration and anger on sin, and Satan, the father of lies (John 8:44, 1 John 3:8). Not on God!

If you truly want to get back at the evil within this world, submit your life to Jesus Christ and spend your time serving Him.

By doing so you will be shining light into this dark world, spreading the Gospel of salvation, amongst the Sea of broken people. And every soul that submits to the one True Almighty God, is one less soul bound to the slavery of sin.

We focus so much on the actions of others, but that is not where our focus should be.

The people's actions are because of their sinful nature, and correcting the actions of a sinful person, only leaves a million other sinful actions to be corrected.

The only TRUE remedy for this broken world is the blood of Jesus Christ. By submitting ourselves to God, the curse of sin is broken through Jesus's work on the Cross, and we move one step forward to the kingdom that we long for.

That kingdom is not of this world, it is a heavenly Kingdom that will set us free from the hurt, pain, and depravity of this broken world.

Chapter 12

Never too Broken for GOD!

Never too Broken for GOD!

What better way to wrap up this journey than to end with stories and testimonies of people that I know? They all have been lifted up and healed from their brokenness by Jesus Christ. We need to see the importance of our testimonies, because, in our weakness, God shows His strength.

Our experiences in life and the consequences we faced because of our sins, or because of the sin of others are important parts of our story.

The scars, hurt, and wounds of this world will sometimes show on us physically, but the joy and the light of God Almighty are within us and are burning bright and shining through the darkness and brokenness of our lives.

By sharing this with others, we can allow the world to see that there is hope in Jesus, no matter how broken we are. This eternal hope lives on and does not fade like the hope the world offers.

I pray that you are encouraged by these testimonies and that it inspires you to share your testimony with others.

Highlighting where you were before knowing the Lord, and then glorifying God for where He has brought you, is beneficial while sharing the Gospel with the Broken World.

Here is only a small glimpse of what God can do in the lives of Broken people when they are willing to accept His call to repentance and salvation through Jesus Christ.

First, let's start with a testimony of a brother in Christ whom I have known my entire life. He was involved in street gangs, crime, and violence. He almost lost his life after being jumped by his own Gang when he was 17 years old. He was filled with Anger, sadness, and despair and felt like he had no way out. He heard the Gospel and was called by the Lord. Through the saving power of the blood of Jesus Christ, his entire life has changed. He now has a wonderful wife, two beautiful children, and a successful business, he became a pastor, an evangelist to the homeless and broken, and has even planted a Church. He continues in ministry to this day and his love for the Lord continues to burn bright within him.

This testimony is from a brother whom I met about a year ago but has become a great friend. His goal in life before being saved was to become a drug dealer, gangster, and player.

Soooo... That's exactly what he did.

He started small but wanted to move up to a bigger game and started trafficking pounds of Marijuana when he was 23 years old. He started making money and it didn't take long for him to start using drugs to kill time, while his friends were working real jobs... He started with Xanax, oxytocin, and lean.

Eventually, the pills became hard to find so he started smoking heroin. Which led him to make worse decisions. That's when fights, shoot-outs, and robberies began.

The robbery of a gun store would be the catalyst that changed his life. This is what got him arrested. While he was in jail, he fell into depression and was completely lost. He dropped to his knees, not knowing the ramifications of what God was about to do for him. He started praying and told God that he couldn't follow Him, because he couldn't see Him, and he even doubted that He was real....

That is when he asked God to prove that He is real.

And if He did, he'd follow Him.

He also promised God that he would be the man that He wanted him to be.

To his surprise, God went to bat for him. Even though he had signed a plea deal for a one-and-a-half-year prison sentence, he miraculously got off with just probation...

How did that happen?

Well, it was because God inspired the man he robbed to show up and speak highly on his behalf and asked the judge to be lenient on him... Wow!!!!

After he was released, he was sitting on his balcony, and it was as if he opened his eyes for the first time.

He could finally see the TRUTH!

The conviction of the Holy Spirit hit him hard, and all the bad things he had done in his life came crashing down on him. He repented and accepted Jesus Christ as his savior and at that moment he knew that he had been forgiven.

It has been eight years since the Lord called him and saved him and it was my great honor to Baptize him last year. He now owns his own business, runs a popular Christian apologetics TikTok channel, and spends his time learning about God and preaching the Gospel to the lost.

Next is a testimony of my sister in Christ whom I have known for almost 7 years. I have had the great privilege of seeing her transformation from Broken to Saved and was blessed to see her Baptism into the Body of Christ. She has had a very difficult life. Both of her parents spent time in prison, while she was a child and she ended up homeless at an early age. She was bouncing from house to house and had to learn to grow up way too soon. As a result of having very little guidance, and direction she became a single mother early on. She suffered from depression, identity issues, and very low self-esteem. She felt alone, hopeless, and broken. The Gospel was shared with her, and the Lord called her into repentance and has enjoyed a relationship with him ever since. She is now glowing with happiness and true joy, knowing that she will never be alone again because the Lord will never leave her, nor forsake her. She teaches her children about the saving grace of God through Jesus Christ and talks to others about her Lord and Savior.

This testimony is from a sister in Christ, who is very near and dear to my heart. She grew up in a loving single-parent home but did not know the Lord.

She became addicted to drugs in high school, and after an extended period of heavy drug use, she was able to get herself clean and was talked into being baptized into the Mormon church. She never felt like that was the truth and ended up leaving the Mormon church and started using again.

She ended up meeting a Man and became pregnant. Not too long into the pregnancy, her unborn child's father was murdered.

She struggled to stay sober while pregnant. And after giving birth she fell into the same old habits. And because of falling back into drugs and bad choices, she ended up spending a year and a half in prison.

After being released from prison she spent the years to come bouncing back and forth between addiction and sobriety. She got mixed up with a man who was an addict · and a criminal. Unfortunately, his lifestyle mixed with her bad choices and drugs led to a very dark path.

She not only became an accomplice to crimes but also was coerced to participate in them. After years of being together in a very toxic relationship, her boyfriend suddenly died, and she ended up being busted by an undercover police officer who spent several years building a major case on her now-deceased boyfriend.

After her arrest and being bailed out of jail by her youngest son and her mother, the cloud of drug use cleared, and she realized that she was in major trouble. She became overwhelmed with depression, and anxiety and felt hopeless with no way out.

She started searching for something more to life in any way she knew how. She got infatuated with spirituality, new-age religions, and Eastern religious practices. She was enticed by the teachings of chakras, energy, and things like that.

That is just about the time she heard the True Gospel of Jesus Christ, and it just so happened to be preached to her by none other than my sister.

To everyone's surprise, she not only was willing to hear the Truth, but she accepted the Gospel with eagerness. She repented from her past debauchery and accepted Jesus Christ as her Lord and Savior.

Unfortunately, this is where I fell short.

To my shame, I thought that she would be unwilling to hear the Truth of the Gospel and thought she was too far gone to be reached...

I have since admitted this to her and offered her my sincere apology.

Since then, God has used me to minister to her, guide her and strengthen her in the word and even had the privilege of being there for her baptism.

We participate in Bible study together, and even though her past crimes have resulted in her imprisonment, we still stay in touch weekly. Her light is stronger than ever, and she accepts that she could not avoid the consequences of her past. She rests assured knowing that she has been delivered from brokenness and judgment, into salvation by the blood of Christ.

She uses her time to openly evangelize while in prison and is shining God's light in that extremely dark place. She has been clean and sober longer than she has been in years.

What is so wonderful about her story is that I have never seen her so happy! She is using every moment that she has, to learn more about the scripture, by diving into deep study. And believe it or not, she is currently working on her certification for Christian doctrine and theology.

She is excited for God to continuously use her throughout the time she has left in prison, but also is excited to see God's plan for her when she is released. She has a heart for evangelism and a great love for the Lord and I'm truly grateful to be able to call her my sister.

This last testimony is from a brother in Christ whom I have known for about 7 years. Unfortunately, he was being consumed by the enticements of this world. His love for what the world had to offer led him down a path of sex, drugs, anger, and despair. The catalyst that pushed him over the edge was a back injury which led him down a dark path of addiction.

Prescription pills grabbed a hold of him tight and they would not let go!

He began spiraling and using more and more pills. It started by trying to numb the physical pain but quickly turned into so much more. Several of us tried on numerous occasions to get through to him, but we could never get past his denial.

Him, spiraling out of control broke my heart....

Watching someone we care about, fall apart in front of us is so hard.

We want to help so badly, but it is completely out of our control. That should be a reminder to us all that even though it's out of our control, nothing is outside of God's.

We knew that prayers were the only shot that he had to recover. It became difficult to even be around him towards the last several months of his addiction because he wasn't even the same person anymore.

But God called him into repentance, and he agreed to listen.

After some time in rehab, he came out clean, sober, and had been baptized. His fire for Jesus was such a beautiful thing to witness. But unfortunately, because his faith was so young and his knowledge of God's word was nonexistent, resulted in him being influenced by some old friends and relapsing. He went back to rehab, and the Lord blessed him with yet another chance at a new start.

He is now clean and sober, very strong in his faith and we have bible study together several times a week. He is reading the Word on his own and is maturing in his faith at an exponential rate. He now has roots, and he knows to lean on God and ask Him for help when he faces trials (James 1:2-5). He has a heart for the Broken and Lost and has been helping lead others to faith in Christ, by both exhibiting his faith and using words of encouragement, and by preaching the Gospel. He helps others who struggle with addiction and tells EVERYONE about his Lord and Savior Jesus Christ!

I shared my testimony with you at the beginning of this book and honestly, there was so much more to my past, that I could fill multiple books on just that.... God has done such great things in my life; I could never scratch the surface of the amount of gratitude that I have for my Lord and Savior Jesus Christ. He has blessed me with the privilege to write two books giving honor and glory to Him. They were written in hopes of strengthening and encouraging other believers, and as a tool for evangelism to those who are lost.

God has called me to a position of leadership within several areas of ministry. I lead a men's Bible study and a Men's ministry. I help in youth ministry and have been called to become an elder at my local Church.

To be clear, I'm not speaking of these things to "boast".

Realistically, none of these are my accomplishments, they are all His!

And to be completely honest, I am still in awe that God chose to use somebody like me to do anything for Him. I'm eternally grateful for whatever He has called me to do for His Glory!

I Praise God for His blessings, and His provisions and I thank him every minute of every day, for what He has done for me and all my brothers and sisters in Christ.

We should now all have a solid biblical understanding that none of us are outside of the Love, Grace, and Forgiveness that God offers through the Sacrifice of Jesus Christ.

I am going to finish our journey as final proof of our deliverance from Brokenness with a quote from Paul's letter to the Colossians 1:15-23, "He (Jesus) is the image of the invisible God, the firstborn of all creation. For by Him all things were created, in heaven and on earth, visible and invisible, whether thrones or dominions or rulers or authorities—ALL things were created through Him and for Him. And He is before all things, and in Him, all things hold together. And He is the head of the body, the Church. He is the beginning, the firstborn from the dead, that in everything He might be preeminent. For in Him ALL the fullness of God was pleased to dwell, and through Him to reconcile to Himself ALL things, whether on earth or in heaven, making peace by the blood of His cross. And you, who once were alienated and hostile in mind, doing evil deeds, He has now reconciled in His body of flesh by His death, in order to present you holy and blameless and above reproach before him, if indeed you continue in the faith, stable and steadfast, not shifting from the hope of the Gospel that you heard, which has been proclaimed in all creation under heaven, and of which I, Paul, became a minister."

So, there it is in BLACK and WHITE...

We are Never too Broken for God!

Closing Prayer

Father God,

We are in awe of you! Lord, you are so great! Your mercy, your kindness, and your love surpass anything that we can understand. We are grateful for all of those that you have called to become our brothers and sisters in Christ. And we pray that you may continue to soften the hearts of others.

Lord, we ask you for strength, wisdom, understanding, discernment, and guidance. Heal our brokenness, forgive us for our stumbling and disobedience, and help us to forgive ourselves, as well as others.

Lord, we feel the world becoming darker, and time is feeling short. But regardless of how much time we as individuals, or the world has, I pray that you may use us, for you, for your glory and to be the light within this dark world. Lord, may you use our testimonies as an encouragement to others, and to show that no one is too broken for you.

We love you, and we give you all praise. We come before you humbly covered in the blood of the Lamb, and it is in the great name of Jesus Christ we pray.

Amen and Amen!

Thank You

Most of all, I would like to thank God. Thank you for blessing me with the opportunity to help others with the knowledge you have revealed to me. You have blessed me and kept me alive for a purpose, and I am grateful that you found me worthy to serve you. I am so humbled to direct people to you and share the Gospel of Jesus Christ.

I would also like to thank my wife. You are my love, my inspiration, my passion, and my drive. Thank you for being an excellent mother to our children and the best wife I could have hoped for!

A special thank you to my parents for putting up with me through tough times and being the parents that God called you to be, you helped mold me into the man I am today. Thank you for guiding me in the right direction, and even when I was lost, your prayers and advice were not in vain.

I want to thank my children for inspiring me to be a better Dad; your innocence and joy bring so much to my life, you have helped me become more selfless, and I thank God for every moment we share.

About The Author

I am just a fellow Brother in Christ, forgiven of my many transgressions, by the Grace of the one True God Almighty, through Faith in the Lord Jesus Christ! I am grateful that God is using me for His Kingdom and His Glory. And I recognize that all the good that has come into, and through my life is only because of Him!

Made in the USA
Columbia, SC
10 November 2024

45811634R00070